Steam Memories: 1950's – 1960's

No. 99: North Eastern Engine Sheds 5

David Dunn

Copyright Book Law Publications 2018

ISBN 978-1-909625-83-9

INTRODUCTION

The engine sheds in the Hull District of British Railways North Eastern Region remained a separate entity under their own code 53 until 1960 when so-called rationalisation reduced their status so that they then fell into a revamped code 50 group with York holding the top spot at 50A, and Hull Dairycoates as 50B, Hull Alexandra Dock as its sub, Hull Botanic Gardens as 50C, and 50D being awarded to Goole. Neither Hull Springhead nor Bridlington figured any more in the great scheme of NE Region engine sheds, or motive power depots as they were now generally titled. Steam was on its way out and only those depots which had been remodelled with diesels in mind or had active steam allocations would survive, initially.

However, let us just backtrack a little to the days when BR was in its infancy and LNER influence was still something to be reckoned with. When Hull Dairycoates was given the prestige of a BR main shed (its gigantic size as a building mattered not a jot to those in authority) and coded 53A with garage shed status given to Botanic Gardens, Springhead (Alexandra Dock being its sub), and Bridlington becoming B, C, and D respectively.

This album does not delve too deep into the history of those Hull District engine sheds – although where necessary reference to certain events will be made – nor does it try to cover pictorially every class of locomotive working from those sheds in BR days. What it does try to reflect is the transition which took place with the buildings themselves, and the motive power therein. Hopefully we have included something for everybody.

Finally, we would like once again to thank the Armstrong Railway Photographic Trust (ARPT) for the use of images illustrated in this album.

David Dunn, Cramlington, 2017

(*Cover*) **See Page 4**

(*Previous page*) **Dairycoates motive power depot, 9th June 1962 with resident 2-6-0s – Ivatt Cl.4 No.43071 and BR Standard No.77000 – stabled around one of the outside turntables at the western end of the rebuilt shed.** *I.S.Carr (ARPT)*.

Printed and bound by The Amadeus Press, Cleckheaton, West Yorkshire

First published in the United Kingdom by Book Law Publications, 382 Carlton Hill, Nottingham, NG4 1JA

53A – DAIRYCOATES

Gresley K3 No.61952 appears to be stabled on the through road between No.5 shed and the outside No.6 turntable. This image allows us a view of the completed gable wall which was built between Nos.5 and 6 roundhouses to allow the isolation of the outside unit. Altogether more than half a million pounds were expended on the alterations at Dairycoates; a sum which nowadays seems minimal but in the post-war years of the 1950s was one heck of a lot of money. The K3 is wearing that all-too-familiar coat of filth which came to be accepted at normal during BR times. No.61952 transferred into Dairycoates on 10th September 1961 from Tweedmouth so was a bit of a 'rare bird' in Hull. This image must have been recorded in 1962 when the 2-6-0 was due a major overhaul. Prepared for a trip to Doncaster shops, the K3 got there only to be condemned in December and shortly afterwards cut-up. *V.Wake (ARPT).*

Before the rebuilding of the roofs: The view through at least three of the five in-line roundhouses on a date to be determined but nevertheless at some time in the 1950s. Having three turntables in view suggests the photographer was standing on No.6 turntable at the extreme western end of the vast building. Identified locomotives include: Resident A7 No.69782 53A which transferred to Tyne Dock 6th March 1955; Bradford B1 No.61031 REEDBUCK which was resident at 37C from 13th May 1951 to 12th January 1958; resident K3 No.61874 which had transferred from Heaton on 12th May 1946 and was condemned 22nd May 1961; resident A7 No.69788 which was another 1946 arrival at Dairycoates and which transferred to Springhead on 16th October 1955. No clear date is emerging but anytime up to and including early 1955 seems a reasonable assumption. The actual rebuilding of the sheds and demolition of the surplus buildings was begun in 1956. *K.H.Cockerill (ARPT).*

The Dairycoates No.6 turntable and three residents 9th June 1962: By now the 53A shed code has been changed to 50B and all of the trio carry plates stating such. The two Ivatt Class 4 2-6-0s were long standing residents of a class which had a long association with Dairycoates throughout the British Railways period. No.43076 had arrived new in October 1950. No.43076 transferred to Royston in October 1965 ending its ties with Hull. No.43069 came second-hand to 53A from Neasden in April 1952 and it too left Hull in 1965 when a transfer to Leeds beckoned in June; withdrawn from Manningham in September 1966 the Cl.4MT was purchased for scrap by Draper's and came back to Hull one last time in December 1966 for cutting-up! WD No.90272 had been around the former LNER area since its purchase from the Government in February 1947. Its first shed was Annesley but on 29th November 1947 it moved into what would become the North Eastern Region of BR at Tyne Dock and remained loyal to that authority until the final days of steam on that region. On 6th February 1949 it made the first of three moves to Dairycoates, moving to York eight months later on 11th October only to return to 53A six weeks later. Nine weeks after that it was back to Tyne Dock for a spell pushing those heavy iron-ore trains up to the steel works at Consett. Exactly one year and sixteen days later a reprieve saw the 2-8-0 transfer south for the final time and a longer association with Dairycoates was begun. That relationship was severed when further examples of the EE Type 3s started to arrive in the spring of 1967. After that it was off to Goole for the WD on 7th May but after just six weeks there the end closed-in and No.90272 was withdrawn. Ironically it returned to Hull one more time when it was towed to Draper's and then cut-up on 18th December 1967. *I.S.Carr (ARPT).*

A WD 2-8-0, No.90704, and K3 No.61874 beneath the coaling plant on 4th April 1954. This appliance was quite innovative when introduced in March 1916 and although designed by the North Eastern Railway it followed North American practice in that a bucket conveyor charged the two overhead 150-ton capacity coal hoppers. Later British practice saw coaling plants which could haul loaded coal wagons up the towers to be discharged directly into bunkers, or plants whereby beneath ground bunkers could be loaded from wagons and then hauled aloft to discharge their contents into overhead bunkers. This Dairycoates plant therefore was quite unique in the United Kingdom and worked for some fifty years before it was finally retired and then demolished in 1967. Each bunker had two coal chutes enabling four tenders to be charged at the same time. Two grades of coal could be stored in the bunkers but that luxury didn't always materialise in BR days when coal quality took a downward turn. *F.W.Hampson (ARPT).*

Another view of the coaling plant, this time from the west; the date is 9th June 1962 and a queue is forming. It is after all a Saturday so most engines have finished work for the weekend therefore there is no rush to process this lot. Oh yes, the engine numbers from the left: 61884, 63666, and 90099; the other 2-8-0 beneath the gantry is O4/3 No.63701 from 41H Staveley (G.C.). *I.S.Carr (ARPT).*

Robinson 04s had not only visited Hull since pre-Grouping days, they had been allocated to both Dairycoates and Springhead from the early LNER era when the company purchased hundreds of them in deals which could only be described as 'no-brainers' in this day and age. The locomotives although second-hand were hardly used and as each month of the post-war years went by, the Government dropped their prices. To top it all, these locomotives were constructed by some of the best engineering firms in the world on Government contracts and the 'icing on the cake' was a superb design which turned out to be robust and long lasting. In early BR days Dairycoates had twenty-odd of the Robinson O4s and a handful of the Thompson rebuilds (Class O1) allocated. *I.S.Carr (ARPT)*.

Isn't this where the diesel shunters normally live? Wearing a new 50B shed plate, resident J94 No.68042 stables on one of the outside roads in one of the now roofless roundhouses on Saturday 9th June 1962. This was the last active J94 still allocated to Dairycoates. *I.S.Carr (ARPT).*

9

Redundant locomotives stabled on the siding alongside the wheel-drop and machine shop on the south side of Dairycoates shed on 9th June 1962. Twelve-years old J72 No.69020 has already had the 50B shed plate removed in anticipation of a transfer to yet another shed; it had only been at Dairycoates a couple of years before diesel shunters muscled-in on the few remaining shunting jobs still available around the city. Darlington shed called the little 0-6-0T in October and it worked there until condemned some three days after Christmas in 1963. *I.S.Carr (ARPT).*

K3 No.61875 undergoes a shed repair beneath the new roundhouse roof on 9th June 1962. Those three cylinders could prove to be a boon when out on the road with a heavy train, but for the shed fitters they were a #!*&$#. So as not to be in the way, the K3's tender has been stabled on the adjacent stall with a redundant breakdown crane. No.61875 came to Dairycoates from Heaton in January 1960 and shortly afterwards attended Doncaster shops for its last General overhaul. This class required major shopping every two years so this K3 was now due such an event. However, this is as near to an overhaul as the 2-6-0 was liable to get. It was condemned on 10th December 1962 during the end of the great K3cull. *I.S.Carr (ARPT).*

56G Bradford Hammerton Street shed had sent this J6 0-6-0 on a fitted freight job to Hull and here it is on 4th August 1956 idling away the weekend stabled inside one of Dairycoates roundhouses. The J6 spent its first thirty-odd years of life working from sheds on the East Coast Main Line but from August 1947 it had variously worked from the three former Great Northern sheds in the West Riding – Ardsley, Bradford, and Copley Hill – and then later transferring to some of the ex-Lancashire & Yorkshire Railway establishments when those depots were brought under the NE Region umbrella. Note how clean this engine is compared to the local charges, obviously there were still some cleaners in Bradford at this time. *C.J.B.Sanderson (ARPT).*

More Doncaster influence visiting Dairycoates: O2 No.63946 gets in the queue for the coaling plant in August 1952. One of the LNER-built examples of Gresley's successful GNR 2-8-0s, the O2 was recently ex-Doncaster 'Plant' and so was showing a resemblance of cleanliness. This particular engine was sent new to Newport shed in North Yorkshire to pit it against the NER Q6 0-8-0s from June 1924 to the end of February 1925 when it transferred to New England and more familiar surroundings. At the time this image was recorded the 2-8-0 was allocated to Doncaster but would transfer to Grantham some eight months later. What of the Newport trials? Nothing appears to have come out of that episode, and none of the class was ever sent there on a permanent basis; the Q5s and Q6s were doing a superb job so why alter the status quo! Shortly after WW2 when the LNER was short of large freight engines like these, they purchased hundreds of Austerity 2-8-0s from the WD and they ended up at Newport; perhaps the O2s venture twenty years beforehand was a prelude for that scenario? No.63946 finished its working days at Retford shed and was condemned on 7th April 1963. *C.J.B.Sanderson (ARPT).*

Sentinel shunters were no strangers to Hull where all the engine sheds housed one or more during the late LNER and early BR period. Therefore, Y1 No.68145's arrival at Dairycoates in July 1955 from West Auckland would not have raised any eyebrows. This image shows No.68145 inside one of the roundhouses on 4th August 1956 after the 0-4-0 had been transferred to Bridlington on 22nd April last. Of course, 53D Bridlington was a sub shed to Dairycoates and therefore its locomotives would gravitate back to the main shed for repairs and examinations which is possibly why the Sentinel was at 53A rather than by the seaside. The Sentinel was sent to the works at Darlington on 7th January 1957 but was not repaired; a week later it was condemned. Dairycoates record of Sentinel shunter residencies shows a number of new examples (N) arriving direct from the makers, and others ending their days at the shed (W) thus – BR numbers used only: Y1 class Nos.68137 – 12/10/39 to 26/12/53W; 68139 – 7/11/42 to 10/9/51W, ex Botanic; 68140 – 7/11/42 to 31/5/54W, ex Bridlington; 68141 – 23/7/29N to 2/4/32 & 12/9/32 to 29/3/41; 68142 – 23/7/29N to 19/11/29 to Botanic; 68148 – 10/1/54 to 19/12/55W, ex Bridlington; 68151 – 4/2/31 to 7/11/42 & 19/9/54 to 8/11/54W; Y3 class Nos.68155 – 22/12/27N to 7/11/42; 68158 – 23/8/29N to 16/9/35; 68160 – 2/10/55 to 29/10/56; 68182 – 20/6/54 to 10/6/56; 68183 – 30/9/51 to 29/9/55. *C.J.B.Sanderson (ARPT)*.

Simmering away in August 1956: N10 No.69096 and J25 No.65655 represent some of the North Eastern' old guard at Dairycoates. The six-coupled tank engine could find work on passenger trains, empty stock movements, trip working, and shunting, at a pinch. Dairycoates had plenty of them at one time or another and some three-quarters of the class had served the Hull shed over the half-century of their existence. No.69096 had been to Dairycoates twice during its lifetime, this latest foray beginning on 14th December 1947 and ending exactly ten years later when the 0-6-2T was condemned on 27th December 1957. In this view No.69096 was days away from attending Gateshead shops for a final General overhaul. The J25 alongside had used up all its work attendance's by now and was living on borrowed time. Transferred from Darlington on the 3rd July 1955, the 0-6-0 was a relative newcomer to 53A; it left the shed for the last time in November 1958 and was condemned at Darlington on arrival into shops on 2nd December. Note the Fowler Cl.3 tank, No.40060, in the background; for which see Botanic Gardens later. *C.J.B.Sanderson (ARPT).*

Lunchtime at Dairycoates: 4th April 1954 with Ivatt Cl.4 No.43100 taking in the spring sunshine. The 2-6-0 arrived new in February 1951, transferred to Copley Hill June 1959, Ardsley in October 1959, then to West Hartlepool where it served virtually until the end of steam on the region but was condemned just beforehand in February 1967. Note the construction of the straight shed which lends itself to the design found in colliery buildings of a period in the 20th Century when austere but solid construction was in vogue, yet this shed was apparently opened in 1876. It is possible that a rebuild of that end wall took place at some time during the LNER period utilising rolled steel joists with brick infills. *F.W.Hampson (ARPT)*.

Yes, we've seen this image or similar beforehand! Nevertheless, it's worth another trip out simply because it is an interesting story surrounding the reason why a Cambridge based B12 should be stabled outside on a stall originally sheltered by No.3 shed at Hull Dairycoates in May 1959. The 4-6-0 was working an excursion from Lincoln to Bridlington when it developed a hot-box; the exact location of the incident is unknown but it must have been nearby. The B12 was taken to Dairycoates for repair on 14th May. Over the next couple of days the errant axle-box was re-lined and then No.61577 worked a couple of local trips to bed-in the lining. It returned to Cambridge on Thursday 21st May none the worse for its ordeal. Note the lack of a shed-plate (it had only just transferred to Cambridge from Norwich). During the following September the Beyer, Peacock-built 4-6-0 was condemned at Stratford works. The new gable of No.4 roundhouse (No.1 now I suppose as only two of them remained) looks impressive whereas the floor of this former roundhouse is a bit of a mess! This area around No.3 turntable was eventually totally refurbished, although left open to the elements, so that diesel shunters could use the stalls for weekend stabling which in turn enabled crews to retrieve their charges quicker – old habits die hard. Finally, for the record, the BR crest worn on the tender of No.61577 is a wrong-facing example applied by Stratford – just thought I'd mention it! *DR Dunn coll (ARPT).*

WD No.90044 standing near the ash pits on 18th December 1966 as though it was waiting to have its fire cleaned or dropped. In actuality some eighteen days beforehand the latter action had been carried out for the final time and the 'Austerity' had been left on this spot on the north side of the shed ever since. Oh yes, No.90044 had been condemned on that same Thursday. There was much to do to prepare the 2-8-0 for the next sequence of events; empty the tender of both coal and water, empty the boiler of water too. However, the lack of personnel to carry out the necessary actions had left No.90044 in limbo – look at all that coal! Of course, it wouldn't really matter because this WD was sold to a certain Mr. Albert Draper and just a few weeks later, in February he had got the locomotive in his yard at Sculcoates where it was demolished as history was being made! Before the 2-8-0s came to Dairycoates – Robinson's, Thompson's, and Riddles examples had all served here – the North Eastern eight-coupled goods engines used to take care of the heavy freight around here. From NER days the Raven 0-8-0s were in residence and during the 1920s they were joined by half a dozen Q10s from the former H&BR. Ten new Q7s started life here at Dairycoates in 1919 but they had all gone by 1928 replaced by ex-ROD O4s. Eighteen Q5s made up some of the heavy freight pool during NER and early LNER days and these were joined by Q6s which during the 1940s numbered more than forty examples at Dairycoates; the last four 0-8-0s were transferred away in December 1949 as the WD 2-8-0s started to find favour. So, over the decades since eight-coupled freight locomotives became the chosen type for heavy goods work, Dairycoates had housed many of their kind, not just in numbers but in various classes too. *A.Ives (ARPT)*.

With nearly three-quarters of the class allocated to Dairycoates in early BR days, and three others residing at Springhead shed, it might be said that the A7 class Pacific tanks basically belonged to Hull. Add a fair number of A6 and A8, not to mention a handful of the T1 4-8-0 tanks and it might be construed that Hull did indeed like its tank engines on the large side. This is No.9773 outside the entrance to No.3 shed (in the background), with No.4 shed on the left. The date is 19th September 1948 and we are stood on the yard of the straight shed which was out of frame to the right. The sand furnace which supplied the whole shed with its requirements was located in the lean-to building against No.3 shed. No.9773 (69773 from 12th March 1949) came to Dairycoates on 12th March 1945 (there is no significance regarding 12th March any year) after an unusual and interesting career which didn't quite follow the normal course for the class. The 4-6-2T started life at Darlington and was put into traffic during December 1910 at Shildon. In March 1925 it moved to York but returned to Shildon two months later. At the end of October it went to Ardsley where it resided for nearly a year before making its way back to Shildon on 1st September 1926. No sooner had it arrived back in the North-East and it was off south again, this time to Doncaster on 21st October 1926. It never went back to work in County Durham again and only visited the area to attend works at Darlington. Some thirteen years were spent by No.1129 (its NER and first LNER number) at Doncaster before heading east to Immingham where more large yards required its presence but just over a month later it went back to Doncaster. Now comes probably the strangest transfer when the big tank was sent to Northwich in Cheshire on 17th July 1939 only to return to Doncaster in time for the Declaration of War. Starbeck was its next port of call but not until 23rd June 1943; plenty of time to help move the heavy munitions trains from the Royal Ordnance Factories in the locale. After that it was Hull. Condemned on 23rd March 1955, No.69773 was cut up at Darlington. Oh yes, they all ended their days at one or other of the Hull sheds – Dairycoates or Springhead that is. *K.H.Cockerill (ARPT).*

One of the rebuilt roundhouses some ten years after the occasion with an array of incredibly clean motive power gathered around the turntable on 18th December 1966. Note the main girder spanning the turntable is a fabricated affair and quite different from the two installed at Botanic Gardens doing the same job from about the same period (see pages 26 and 28) although the depths of the girders appear similar, this example – an exact mirrored image was spanning the void to the photographers left – consists a multitude of girders and steel beams of varying profiles; concrete beams carry the flat roof over the side stalls. The original 60ft turntables were left in situ at Dairycoates and this appliance (it looks like No.5 turntable) still has the guard rails around its periphery. Normally these turntable guard rails got damaged on a daily basis and were either replaced or latterly left off completely. So what of the locomotives which consists a WD at either end, with three B1s in the middle? No.90016 had been at Hull (Dairycoates) – according to the legend on the bufferbeam – since transferring from West Hartlepool on 13th March 1966 [the painted legend was applied during a Non-Classified visit to the works at Cowlairs during the previous summer]. The 2-8-0 was about to vacate Hull altogether and was transferring to Goole on this very Sunday. No.90016 returned to Hull in 1968 courtesy of the purchasing power of Albert Draper who cut it up in their Neptune Street premises. Thompson B1 No.61306 had started its BR career at Dairycoates, arriving new from the NBL Co. in April 1948. It quickly re-allocated to Botanic Gardens but when that depot was modernised for diesel railcar use it returned to 53A in June 1959. When Dairycoates was threatened, the 4-6-0 transferred on 25th June 1967 to Low Moor where it was condemned on the last day of September 1967; it was purchased for preservation shortly afterwards. No.61255 transferred to Hull from Thornaby on 4th March 1962 and remained at Dairycoates until withdrawn on 24th June 1967. No.61289 was also ex-Botanic on 14th June 1959 and it too succumbed on 24th June 1967. WD No.90378 had been associated with Dairycoates shed since being purchased by the LNER in August 1947; except for five weeks at York in 1949, the 'Austerity' had flitted between Dairycoates and Springhead no less than seven times during the 1950s. Once Springhead closed to steam No.90378 settled down at Dairycoates for almost nine years before moving on to Sunderland on 17th June 1967; it was condemned three months later. *A.Ives (ARPT).*

K3 No.61902 and her peers outside the straight shed in 1959. Behind our subject is the wheel drop building with its doors ajar; a filthy WD awaits entry to the machine shop. It mustn't be forgotten that Dairycoates shed had a huge allocation for most of its life and these were made up from all sorts of classes from the lowliest tank engines to the 2-8-0 goods engines encompassing classes O1, O4, and WD. The K3s and B1s made up the cream of the mixed traffic types which could do virtually anything but excelled at speed. When BR came into being the shed could boast twenty-odd K3s and that remained about the norm until the class was rather rapidly broken up over the four year period from 1959 to 1962! No.61902 – 61965 stables to the left – had been allocated to Dairycoates since 23rd July 1945 after working its way from Tyneside during the war years. It was one of the 1961 casualties being condemned on 3rd July, and then cut up at Doncaster. No.61965 survived until 3rd December 1962 and was one of the last to go. *A.R.Thompson (ARPT).*

WD No.90008 inside the rebuilt No.4 roundhouse on Sunday 18th December 1966: This 2-8-0 had a long history with Dairycoates having transferred from Tweedmouth on 16th May 1951 (it had actually been at 53A since 6th February 1949 but had gone to the border town just before Christmas for six-month stint). Note that the 50B shed plate is absent whilst the engine is quite 'clean-ish' especially for a 'Dub-Dee' at this period on BR, at Dairycoates! Withdrawal for this engine was some four months away on 10th April 1967 so the lack of a shed plate must be down to souvenir hunters. Perhaps the plate on No.90016 might be fitted when that WD leaves the shed for the last time? Dairycoates engine shed has hosted no less than eighty-one WD 2-8-0s over the years when the locomotives worked over Britain's railways. The first LNER examples arrived in 1947 but beforehand many of the class visited Hull whilst on loan to the LNER pre-D-Day. They were rugged, simple, tough, and strong. Ideal for the heavy freight work on which they seemed to thrive. They were cursed by those who manned them and also by those who maintained them but they just kept going when finer precision tools gave-in. That none of the 733 BR examples were preserved is a shame but strange things were happening when the end of steam came: Pannier tanks were being given life-saving status; as were the 'Manors' 'Stanier Class 5s' Gresley A4s, 'West Country' and 'Merchant Navy' Pacifics. Whichever way you look at it the preservation movement during those early days went slightly adrift. Of course, regrets started to surface once certain classes had disappeared for good: Peppercorn A1 and Gresley K3 for instance. Luckily the Swedes had not quite been so short-sighted as BR and because of them we now have a working WD 'Austerity' 2-8-0, albeit with a modern copy tender, running in Yorkshire of all places – where else?! *A.Ives (ARPT)*.

A visit to Dairycoates on Saturday 10th April 1965 found the following locomotives 'on shed:'

Ivatt Cl.4 2-6-0:	43069, 43077, 43078.
Thompson B1 4-6-0:	61010, 61012, 61255, 61289.
WD 2-8-0:	90008, 90030, 90042, 90092, 90099, 90213, 90265, 90272, 90352, 90452, 90462, 90478, 90586, 90677.
0-6-0DM shunter:	D2081, D2102, D2157.
0-6-0DE shunter:	D3070, D3080, D3081, D3232, D3234, D3675.
EE Type 3 Co-Co:	D6730, D6734, D6736, D6739, D6740, D6741, D6775, D6782.
0-6-0DE shunter:	12113, 12114, 12115, 12118.

On the dump (Seven Section) were Nos: 45597, 60126, 61031, 61165, 61179, 62020, 62033, 62040, 62066, and 62070. These were all awaiting haulage to Draper's scrapyard at nearby Sculcoates*.

Resident WD 2-8-0 90008 was attached to the depot's snowplough, the weather still unpredictable in the fourth month of the year!

An analysis of the locomotives present shows that the diesels were by now entrenched, especially the shunting types which had ousted steam on all the remaining yard work and Paragon pilot jobs in Hull after many years of residency. It is interesting to note the three distinctly different shunter types: the 204 h.p. 0-6-0 Diesel Mechanical, the 350 h.p. 0-6-0 Diesel Electric, and the older BR type of 350 h.p. 0-6-0DE which were the immediate forerunners of the shunters which were to become TOPS Class 08. Main line diesel locomotives were represented by Dairycoates own resident fleet of English Electric Type 3s – D6730 to D6741 – which came new in late 1961 onwards to June 1962 – and then second-hand D6775 from Thornaby in June 1964, preceded by D6779 and D6783 in late 1962. Eight of them, it will be noted, were at home on the day of the visit; others were noted at Goole and Doncaster. They were joined during February and March 1967 by D6784 to D6795. In March 1968 another useful locomotive type, the English Electric Type 1, Nos.D8310 to D8315 transferred from Thornaby but moved away in 1969. Steam was represented by just three classes: ex-LMS Ivatt Class 4 2-6-0s, Thompson B1 4-6-0s – the only former LNER design still 'on the books' at 50B. The WD 2-8-0s constituted the largest number of steam types with fourteen examples on shed; their presence all over the former North Eastern Region was a testimony to their robust design which enabled them to keep going in traffic when other types would have been incapacitated. Amazingly the Peppercorn K1s 2-6-0s filling the sidings on Seven Section, en route to Draper's, were probably in better mechanical condition than the WD 2-8-0s but by some quirk of the period, any defect, major or minor, was enough to get locomotives withdrawn at some depots.

* The Draper's scrapping operation as regards BR steam locomotives was in its infancy at this time, the first examples not having arrived at Seven Section from sheds other than Dairycoates until the previous 8th November when A1 No.60147, and Peppercorn K1s Nos.62058 and 62063 were dumped. During September 1964 some seven withdrawn Dairycoates B16s had accumulated at Seven Section along with a Thompson B1 (the first locomotive dealt with at Sculcoates was B16 No.61420 some seven months earlier) and it was this batch which started the continuous stream of withdrawn locomotives passing through the siding en route to Sculcoates.

By 1965 the shed alterations had been completed, the remaining turntables which were still covered had been given new roofs, those left open to the elements were at each end of the one-time six turntable shed building. This is one of the semi-covered outside 50ft. turntables at the east end of the depot (the former No.3 shed) where diesel shunters could be found in abundance at weekends; the short radiating roads could manage the shunting diesels comfortably but anything longer would be struggling. The four shunters are of the 350 h.p. 0-6-0DE type but of varying vintages with No.12121 identified on the left with 12118 next to it (the detail differences are subtle indicating different workshops involved in overhauls). Dairycoates had ten of these early BR-built locomotives, with most of them sub-shedded at Alexandra Dock and only returning to Dairycoates for examinations. In the background a pair of the depot's EE Type 3 fleet are stabled on the roads feeding into what were the depot's repair sheds and which consisted two straight road buildings with a wheel-drop shed (its centre-glazed pitched roof is still in good condition in this photograph) tagged on. To give some idea of the original layout of the roundhouses here, the No.2 shed was attached on the left of this image, No.1 shed was located obliquely to the south-east of No.2, immediately east and behind the repair shops. Nos.4, 5, and 6 sheds were located to the right although by now only Nos.4 and 5 were sheds in the proper sense of the word, and No.6 was open to the elements, its 60ft. turntable no longer occupied by steam locomotives having been lifted. *Gordon Turner/GD/ARPT.*

Darlington built Class 11 No.12117 was amongst another congregation stabled around No.3 turntable on another weekend at Dairycoates. Dairycoates batch of these shunters numbered 12113 to 12122, all of which were built at Darlington and came new to Hull during the late summer of 1952. All of them had transferred away by the beginning of 1969 although a couple of them had been withdrawn at Dairycoates beforehand. Those that did move away remained within what became the Eastern Region as a whole encompassing the North Eastern Region too. Immingham and Stratford were the main recipients. Note that 12117 has two three-link couplings at the front, one fixed, the other available to be used in situations where such equipment was either broken or missing altogether on vehicles being shunted! This Class 11 was withdrawn in February 1969 at Immingham and was sold for scrap to Arnott & Young at Parkgate where it was broken up in October 1969. Besides these Class 11 0-6-0DEs, Dairycoates had some twenty-seven of the Class 08 derivatives working from the depot over the years; the first of those was D3070 which arrived on 12th November 1953 and was put to work at Alexandra Dock almost immediately. *Gordon Turner/GD/ARPT.*

53B - BOTANIC GARDENS

Upheaval at Botanic Gardens on 4th August 1956; the two roundhouses were undergoing modernisation which was basically a total rebuild. The job was being done piecemeal with sections of the shed being stripped of their roof – the two turntable areas were tackled first – then rebuilt using steel columns to carry steel girders which were supporting precast concrete beams which in turn were covered with cladding and sheet glass – No.2 shed only; No.1 shed because it did not now have a turntable did not require the great arched roof of a turntable shed and therefore a much more modest structure would eventually emerge. Whilst all this was being achieved, the No.2 roundhouse remained active with only small sections occasionally put out-of-bounds whilst the builders got on with their work. This view on the north side of No.2 shed shows Dairycoates based N10 No.69108 standing amongst the cinders and ash stacked either side of the 55ft pit, with building materials. It must be admitted that although it appears that chaos was the order of the day, in reality the planning had ensured something of a smooth transition from old to new with a lot of activity between. The newly completed arch over the No.2 turntable is ready for its end gable wall at this end; on the right can be seen a section of the original 1901 shed whilst beyond the new shed section is the void yet to be filled with a lower roof section over the area where No.1 turntable was located up to just a few months beforehand. The general idea behind the rebuilding was to create a new roundhouse with turntable and stalls where No.2 shed stood (the roundhouses were in fact square but adjacent with no separating party wall) basically a refurbished example of what already existed with a new shed. The No.1 shed was to have its turntable and pit removed, stalls filled in and a shed with straight roads was to replace it whilst the building was of a different profile to the new No.2 shed. However, things were to change, radically! *C.J.B.Sanderson (ARPT).*

Botanic Gardens had done well on the coaling stage front with this manual stage being replaced in 1932 by the mechanical plant visible on the left. An earlier coal stage at the entrance to No.1 shed had in turn been replaced by this stage on a date unknown, and for reasons unknown – that space was latterly levelled and occupied by a water tank. As can be seen, the pre-1932 structure was certainly well made with massive concrete foundations topped with a substantial brick wall on its west side – the bitterly easterly winds were allowed to enter the front of the stage unbridled! Beneath the stage were rooms occupied by platelayers; blacksmiths; a joiner; the Sentinel fitter (installed since 1929 to maintain the railcars as no shunter types were allocated to Botanic; by 1946 he was no longer required); and a store. Note in this August 1956 image that wagons are still stabled on the coaling stage simply to keep them out of the way. Of course occasionally the mechanical coaling plant would require maintenance and then the manual stage would come into its own again. The coaling plant was supplied and built by Babcock & Wilcox Ltd., and commissioned in 1932 at a time when the railways were trying to modernise certain operations and cut down on staff and at the same time, the Government were giving grants and loans to the railway companies to enable them to function more efficiently and ironically keep more people in jobs! The engineering firms were in turn helped with financial incentives to keep people employed. The plant had just one bunker as really only one grade of coal was required and that was for passenger engines; there were however two feed chutes. With this type of plant the loaded wagons (20-ton max.) were lifted up the side of the plant and when above the bunker top they were tipped and their contents fell directly into the bunker. There were restrictions on the size of wagons used, mainly a minimum size, and it was take 2 minutes 5 seconds to hoist a loaded wagon and 1 minute 20 seconds to lower the empty. BR Standard Cl.3 No.77000 had only been allocated to Botanic since July 1955 along with sisters No.77001, and 77010. They were gone by the time the diesel railcars came en masse in September 1959. *C.J.B.Sanderson (ARPT).* 27

Back at No.2 roundhouse on that 4th day of August 1956, we meet a couple of the residents seemingly leading a precarious existence on the stalls leading off the electric turntable. A5 No.69811 had spent most of its life on the former GC lines working from Neasden but had come north when Thompson L1s had nudged her and her sisters off the Marylebone suburban services. Initially Saltburn was the recipient for this 4-6-2T in June 1950 but it was transferred to Botanic Gardens on 19th August 1951. It turned out to be the A5's last shed but withdrawal was in the future – at some time during October 1958. Above the A5 the original shed roof hangs on but soon that too will be demolished. A8 No.69860 was a newcomer of sorts having arrived at the end of the previous September; it would be gone in June 1957 back to its old hunting ground at Middlesbrough. It was actually second time around at Botanic for this big tank; it spent four years here during WW2. Above the locomotives can be seen the girders newly employed to hold up the new roof. The girders had come from Dorman Long at Middlesbrough so had something in common with the A8. The cameraman is standing in what was formerly No.1 roundhouse which was soon to become a straight shed. From here on things got complicated because even though diesel railcars (DMUs) were being introduced and reservation for their servicing etc. was being made here at Botanic, it was soon realised that the full length of both rebuilt roundhouses would be required to house them. The rebuilding carried on with the twin sheds but on the ground things now took a turn. To add fuel to the fire, Dairycoates was also going through rebuilding and rationalisation whereby only two of its original roundhouses were required as the end of steam was actually being acknowledged. So there we have it. What to do with Botanic Gardens engines whilst the change takes place? It was to be 13th June 1959 before the converted shed at Botanic was handed over for diesel use. In the meantime let's look round the shed for some other nuggets. *C.J.B.Sanderson (ARPT).*

Another view of the two Pacific tanks this from the covered turntable on that August day in 1956. *C.J.B.Sanderson (ARPT).*

Nearly there! Although Botanic Gardens had two internal turntables, it was also blessed with a 50ft diameter open table in the south-eastern corner of the yard adjacent to the shed entrance from the junction at Argyle Street. In early 1955, before the shed rebuilding and alterations started in earnest, D49 No.62754 THE BERKELEY took advantage of the facility after running in from Paragon station and passenger duty; note that the table was man-powered. This 4-4-0 had arrived at Botanic Gardens shortly after the end of WW2 after transfer from York on 8th October 1945. It was to prove to be its last posting for the D49 which had worked from East Riding sheds for the whole of its life except for the war years spent at York. No.62754 was condemned on 3rd November 1958 at Darlington and was then broken at those workshops. *C.J.B.Sanderson (ARPT).*

A few minutes later the D49 has been stabled on the stub line coming off the turntable and can be seen alongside a rather smart looking Thompson L1 No.67763. Just about half-way through its life, the 2-6-4T appears to be getting ready for working some rush-hour traffic; with the oil can, and rag on the running plate and the refill can on the ground, the driver was momentarily stood alongside the photographer Cecil Sanderson so as not to spoil the image. In June 1956 the L1 transferred to Middlesbrough and then, on 30th November 1962, whilst working at Ardsley shed, it was condemned. Six months later it went to Darlington for scrap; lifetime mileage for its thirteen years in service – 397,929, which isn't too bad at all. Note the time on the shed clock states eight minutes to four – dead-on! *C.J.B.Sanderson (ARPT)*.

This is ex-LMS Fowler Cl.3 mixed traffic 2-6-2T No.40059 tucked away at the back of No.2 roundhouse on Sunday 28th August 1955. Note that the central section of the three pitched roofs covering the shed has been removed ready for the rebuilding process to start; a similar event has yet to overtake No.1 shed where the wing-sections on either side of the centre section had also to be removed because that shed was planned to have its turntable removed altogether at this stage of the rebuild. And now for something completely different! The story of the ex-LMS Fowler tanks has oft' been told but it's worth a re-run here to bring those readers unaware of the tale up-to-speed so to speak. The 3MT illustrated was one of eight of her kind which came to Botanic Gardens shed during the previous thirteen months (arriving during the period July to December 1954): Nos.40012, 40017, 40045, 40056, 40057, 40059, 40060, and 40061. Six of them came from Lees shed near Oldham and were motor-fitted as No.40059 featured. The other two came from Trafford Park (40017), and Willesden (40045). They didn't do much at Hull, nothing exciting that is; they managed the duties they were given and were basically 'put-up-with' but they were destined to move on sooner rather than later. It's on record that two at least worked from Bridlington for a time – No.40012 April to December 1956, and No.40060 from October 1955 to April 1956. Nos.40045 and 40059 were the first to leave Hull and they transferred to Neville Hill in June 1956. The rest moved en masse to Rugby in December 1956 (the two Leeds examples followed them to 2A), and that was the end of that particular saga. *F.W.Hampson (ARPT)*.

D49 No.62741 THE BLANKNEY stabled on a stall off the No.2 turntable on 28th August 1955. Note that the No.1 shed roof is still intact but not for much longer. Also note that the shed appears bereft of locomotives so work must have been about to start on the demolition of the roof. Not mentioned already but perhaps noted by certain readers, the outside walls of the complete shed, which were in good condition, were left in situ. So, why was the 4-4-0 looking so smart when everything else around here was, well, filthy?! No.62741 had just returned from a General overhaul at Darlington (13th July to 13th August 1955), its penultimate repair. A resident of Botanic Gardens since 12th May 1946, No.62741 had spent the war years on Tyneside working from Gateshead but prior to November 1940 it was based at York from new. It would see the rest of its working life operating from 53B, and was condemned on 30th October 1958. *F.W.Hampson (ARPT).*

In between duties, one-off G5 No.67340 poses with her crew in the shed yard during August 1952. Push-pull fitted just before WW2, the 0-4-4T had extensions fitted to her side tanks in early 1938 during a three-and-a-half-month long 'General' at Darlington. The reason for the extended tanks was to increase water capacity by some 220 gallons so that G5 class could be used in place of diesel railcars on certain routes. As No.387, the 0-4-4T was trialled between Hull and Pontefract, and Hull to York in 1938 but nothing came of the trials for which No.387 was loaned to Botanic from Sunderland; it left Hull for South Blyth in June 1938 but was unaltered as illustrated here. The G5 returned to Botanic Gardens – ex–Starbeck – in April 1942 for a twelve and a half year residency after which it returned to South Blyth for another four years of work there. *C.J.B.Sanderson (ARPT).*

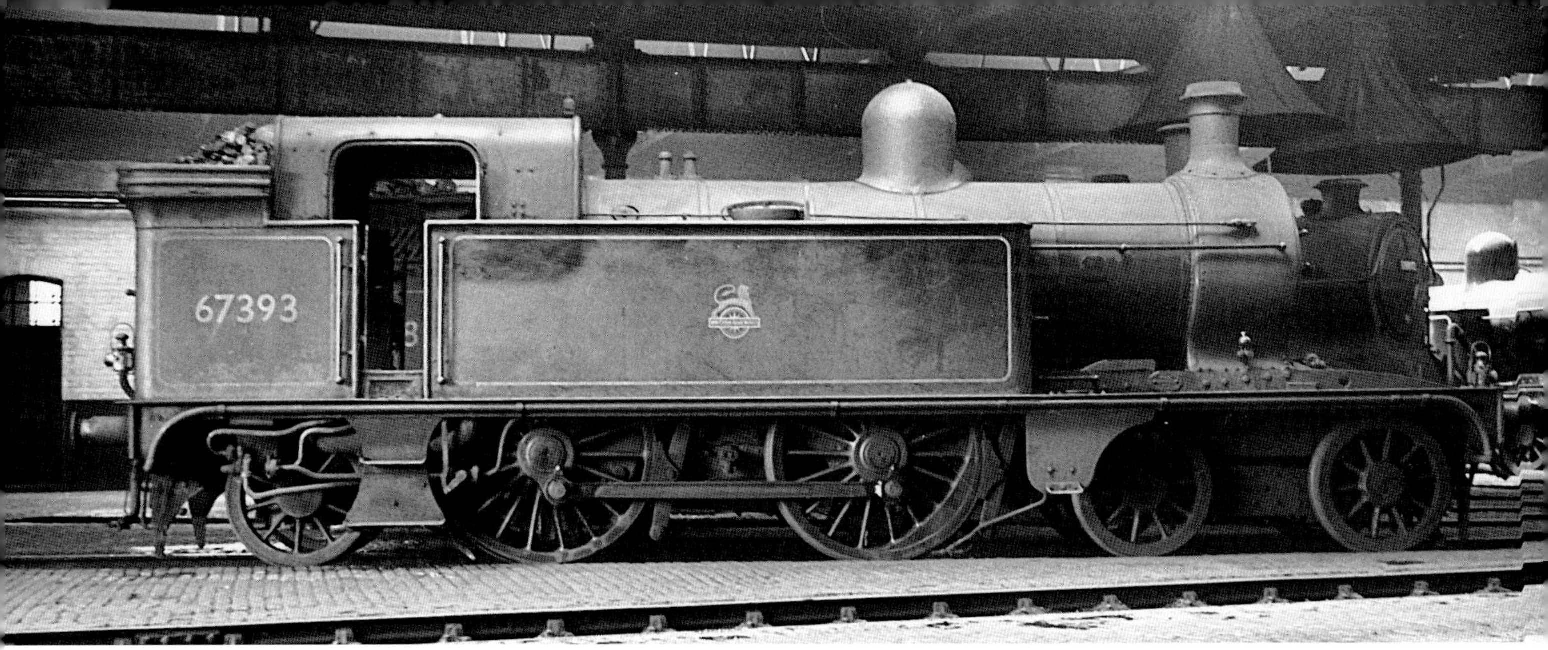

(*above*) Bordering on one of the best looking tank engine designs of all-time was the C12. No.67393 had come from Bradford in June 1931 and then stayed as a resident of Botanic Gardens for the rest of its life. This 18th May 1952 view shows the 'Atlantic' tank during its final year of existence. Already forty-five years old, No.67393 would return to its birthplace in April 1953 and be broken up, surplus to requirements. (*below*) Another fairly long-term resident was G5 No.67282 seen in August 1952 – its tenth year at Botanic – and shortly after return from a 'General' at Gateshead (9th June to 1st July). This G5 had spent the whole of its life working from sheds in Yorkshire and was to continue down that road until condemned on 13th May 1957. *Both C.J.B.Sanderson (ARPT).*

Dairycoates based Ivatt Cl.4 No.43131 stabled on the original coaling stage site in the south yard, outside No.1 shed at Botanic Gardens on Sunday 4th April 1954; time 1420 or twenty past two depending on your preferences! Now what was a 53A 2-6-0 doing at 53B on a Sunday afternoon – stabling of course because there was nowhere else to go. Besides this example, there were others from the Dairycoates Ivatt Class 4 batch spending Sunday at Botanic but without any visit record we can't say which so take your pick from the following: Doncaster-built No.43053 was the first to show up at 53A in August 1950, followed by Darlington built Nos.43076 to 43079 some two months later. Darlington sent another batch, Nos.43099 to 43103 during February and March 1951 but the largest batch came from Horwich between August and November 1951 when Nos.43122 and 43124 to 43131 turned up. They were useful locomotives, and reliable; some would say ugly but they were easy to maintain. Others came to Dairycoates during the period in question and most of these moved on elsewhere. For the record, the works at Doncaster turned them out for £12,565 all in; Darlington for £12,843, and Horwich for £13,316, although No.43127 cost £13,805 because of some special reversing gear! No.43131 was the only one of her kind to remain loyal to Dairycoates and spent the whole of its life allocated to the depot from November 1951 to December 1963. Of course it's time at 53B didn't count. Note the ladder pitched to the roof gully already – it's started! *F.W.Hampson (ARPT).*

Even in August 1956 they were turning up at Botanic Gardens! No.43053 looking fairly normal for the period in dirty/grey/black/limescale cream (Dairycoates livery perhaps but some might argue it was more of a Gateshead hue!); basically BR motive power across the board – clean when ex-works or new, filthy thereafter! This view of the west side of the shed shows the massive water tower built on part of the site of the original coaling stage. Whatever the size of the standard tank plates were, the tank itself was nine long, six wide, and two high. Perhaps someone can enlighten us as to the actual capacity in gallons, and the weight atop that brick edifice; give us the dimensions and we'll do the rest! For the record the Ivatt Cl.4 transferred away from Dairycoates in June 1959 to Low Moor; then West Hartlepool in October. It returned to Yorkshire in September 1963, to Manningham where it resided until April 1964 when withdrawal took place. Sister 43054 which was one of the latecomers to Dairycoates remained in Hull until 1966 when it transferred away to the West Riding. *C.J.B.Sanderson (ARPT).*

A quick look at the 'older order' at Botanic Gardens: D20 newcomer No.62381 (ex-Selby 10th June 1956) which was not looking its best in this August 1956 view stables behind the manual coaling stage. The 4-4-0 wasn't going to be here for too long and in September 1957 it transferred to the 'spiritual' final home of all D20s – Alnmouth! *C.J.B.Sanderson (ARPT)*.

Now what is it keeping this thing going? Resident G5 No.67337 tries to blend in amongst the ash piles in the shed yard at Botanic on 4th August 1956. Fifty-five years old, at least eighteen major overhauls under its belt, thirteen boilers, and nine lives. For this 0-4-4T it was almost over, almost; on 16th December next it was transferred to Middlesbrough who promptly put it into store awaiting works. It got to Darlington at the end of February and two weeks later was condemned by the works and broken up. This view of the shed yard reveals the lines curving off to the left and leading to West Parade junction and then Paragon station. *C.J.B.Sanderson (ARPT)*.

Left and right hand side views of D20 No.62397 at Botanic on 4th August 1956. The 4-4-0 appears to be going off shed to a job at Paragon – most probably a passenger working back home to Bridlington (the topped-up tender is the clue) to which shed it was on loan from Neville Hill for the summer. The D20 was now in the final year of its life, a visit to Darlington in the following January would see it condemned. The tender was the first of ten to undergo rebuilding and in May 1949 it emerged from the shops with a new body on the existing chassis; the body was based on the LNER 3500 gallon standard tender. *Both C.J.B.Sanderson (ARPT)*.

Let's return to the rear (north end) of the shed (No.2) on 28th August 1955 where two A5s were lurking: Nos.69835 and 69836. Now just look at those chimneys! No.69835 has the standard (for the class) built-up flower-pot chimney whereas sister No.69836 had recently acquired (April 1955) a taller chimney as fitted to the Part 1 members of the class. For both engines this had been their first residency at Botanic Gardens and for 69835 its only term which lasted three years and a week exactly; No.69836 had actually arrived in July 1952 and spent five years at 53B but after a three month spell at Darlington it returned to Hull on 15th September 1957 and worked out its days at Botanic Gardens until condemnation on 25th August 1958 during a trip to the works at Darlington. The year of 1958 was to prove a bad one for the NE Region members of the class when all of them were withdrawn. *F.W.Hampson (ARPT)*.

Let us finish off this sequence at Botanic Gardens with another namer: Thompson B1 No.61010 WILDEBEESTE, literally up to its wheel rims in ash and char and firebox debris, looks nothing like what Edward Thompson envisaged when he introduced these 4-6-0s in 1942. The date is 4th August 1956 and this particular B1 is due a period in shops but it would be the end of the year before a trip to works took place and that visit was only for a Casual Light repair which usually meant accident damage repairs. No.61010 was the first of the 1946 batch of B1s built at Darlington and put into traffic in November that year; the North British Locomotive Co. had already delivered No.1040 ROEDEER and dozens more up to No.1093 by then. Our subject here spent the whole of its life working from Hull sheds: Botanic from 2nd November 1946 to 14th June 1959, and Dairycoates until condemned on 7th November 1965 – aged nineteen years! It was sold during the following December to Albert Draper for scrap and made the short journey to Sculcoates yard during February 1966. After two months of dealing with some twenty-three WD 2-8-0s, the B1 was the first ex-LNER engine of the new-year to be cut at Sculcoates – it certainly wasn't the last! *C.J.B.Sanderson (ARPT).*

53C – SPRINGHEAD

An undated view of the western end of Springhead shed circa 1950. Obviously a weekday, the shed is virtually bereft of locomotives, the few inside the building are either receiving maintenance or awaiting their next duty. The gentlemen stood outside are apparently management and staff acknowledging an unknown event out on the main line passing the depot. The eight-road shed was built in 1885 for the opening of the Hull & Barnsley Railway but extensions were added over the next twenty years so that by 1906 the building was some 390ft long and nearly a 100ft wide. Coaling facilities here consisted a stage built at the western end of the depot with a turntable to complete the servicing assets. The site was also home to the H&B locomotive workshops, along with their carriage and wagon departments. The shed closed to steam on 15th December 1958 but what remained of the allocation had vacated the premises at the end of November heading to Dairycoates. Most of the shed had been roofless for some years but in 1955 four of the eight roads were refurbished to temporarily house and maintain the diesel multiple units which had been consigned to the Hull area and which would eventually be housed in the purpose-built diesel depot being created out of the rebuilt shed at Botanic Gardens. It was July 1961 before Botanic was fully operational and able to take the DMUs and the handful of diesel shunters which had relied on Springhead for so long. *K.H.Cockerill (ARPT)*.

Even by 1951 the shed roof was disappearing leaving a forest of iron and steel hanging above the allocation. This 29th July 1951 image reveals resident A7 No.69774 wearing one of the new 53C shed plates; the act that it had attended main works at Darlington just twelve months beforehand for a General and a repaint is totally lost. This Pacific tank had transferred to Springhead from Starbeck in March 1945 and 53C turned-out to be its last shed before withdrawal on 23rd August 1954. WD 2-8-0 No.79227 (90688 from October 1951) was another resident arriving in June 1950 from Dairycoates and remaining loyal to Springhead until that December 1958 purge on steam. Springhead was home to fifty-seven of these 2-8-0s during the twelve years that the shed had them on the books. No.90688 stayed loyal to Hull and was allocated to Dairycoates (Immingham and Tyne Dock were its first sheds in 1947-49, then York for a month in 1949) both before and after its sojourn at Springhead; it was finally ousted on 2nd May 1967 and sent to Goole where condemnation took place seven weeks later. Just to cement the long standing association with its 'adopted' city, the WD was purchased for scrap by Draper's who broke it up in their Neptune Street yard in January 1968. *F.W.Hampson (ARPT).*

44

Another A7/WD combination beneath the transverse roof pitches of naked steelwork at Springhead. The date is 18th May 1952 – a Sunday – and No.69780 along with No.90627 is a Dairycoates charge. Neither engine is tallowed down nor sporting any hessian covers' on their chimneys so storage is probably out of the question. It couldn't have been building work at Dairycoates driving the locomotives to Springhead so what was it on this sunny weekend? *C.J.B.Sanderson (ARPT).*

Shunting engines of Class J72, headed by No.69001, are all facing east inside the shed at Springhead on 24th August 1952. Note that a section of the shed roof is still intact at the western end. *J.W.Armstrong (ARPT)*.

From circa 1930 Springhead shed could call on the facilities of the adjacent but redundant locomotive works for any prolonged repair jobs. Here G5 No.67340 from Botanic Gardens makes use of the facility circa 1952 along with a pair of WD 2-8-0s. Two electrically powered 40-ton capacity overhead cranes were available for those awkward jobs whilst a 5-ton capacity crane was useful for the smaller jobs. *K.H.Cockerill (ARPT).* 47

This 4th August 1956 view inside the 'redundant' locomotive shops reveals Dairycoates A7 No.69786 undergoing some piston valve work. Just to get to the job we can see that the front bogie has been taken out (those 40-ton cranes were useful) and coupling rods removed. In actuality this A7 was allocated to Springhead but nobody had bothered to remove the 53A shed plate before or after the 25th March 1956 transfer. Assuming No.69786 was put back together, and sent out to work it was condemned on 16th December 1957 and afterwards cut up at Darlington. Before we switch our attention, take a look at the buffers worn by the A7! Now then, what about WD No.90429, what is happening there? First thing to notice is the slaking pipe hanging out of the cab window on the fireman's side – why was this action such a common occurrence with the Dub-Dees? Next we have the firebox cloth cladding and its sheet-metal cover drawn back. No.90429 was a Springhead engine, transferring from Mexborough on 29th August 1948. The WD moved back inland on 15th September 1957 when Wakefield beckoned with another ten years' service on offer! So, it all looks rather untidy but the Springhead fitters would soon sort things out. *C.J.B.Sanderson (ARPT).*

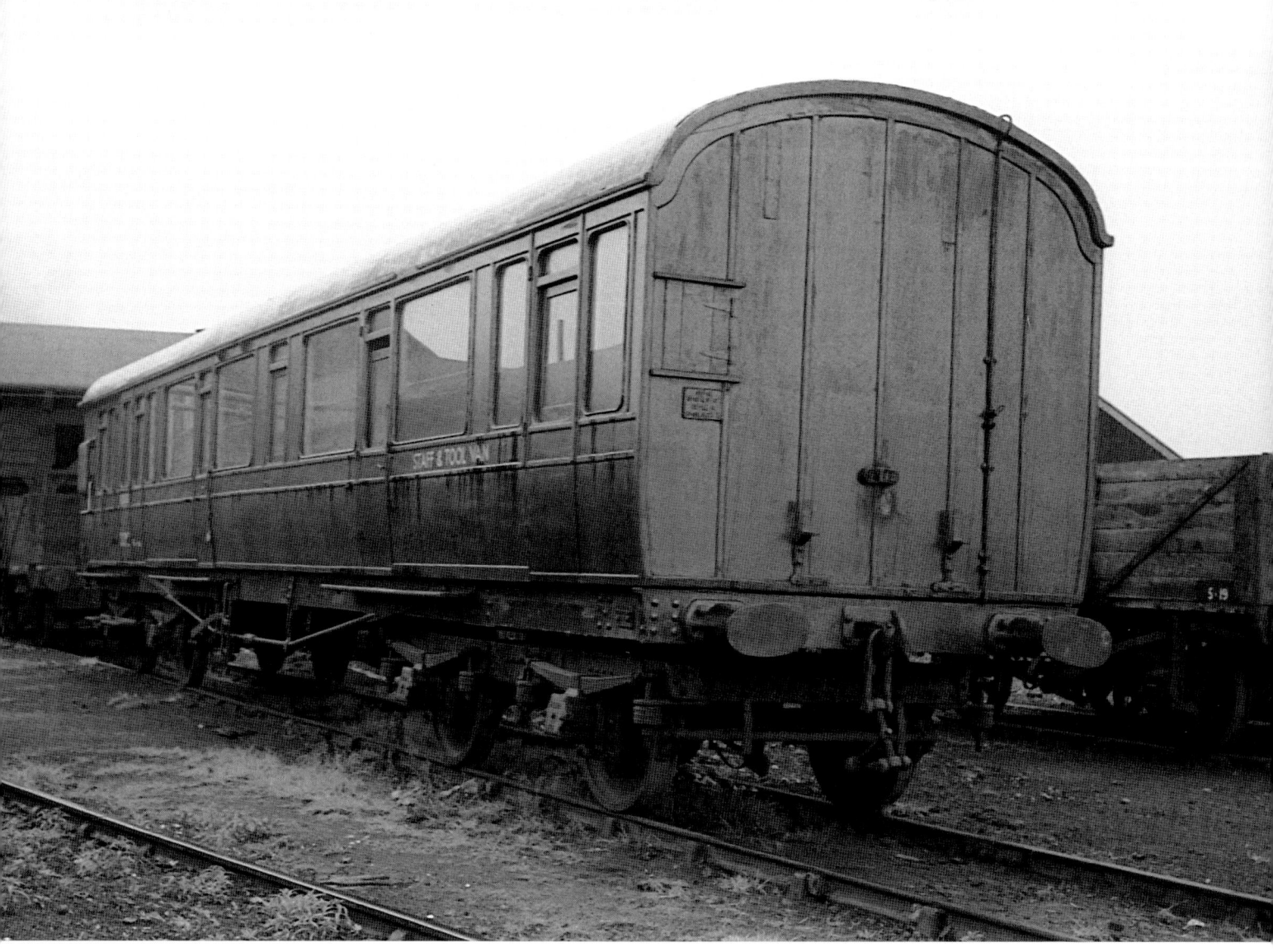

Could this be the Springhead breakdown train or at least part of it? The vehicle is ex-H&B but its present, and past, numbers are not available for the record. The only markings discernible are: STAFF & TOOL VAN. The date: 4th August 1956, note the unseasonable rain! *C.J.B.Sanderson (ARPT).*

Because of its H&B/NER/LNER/BR (up to 1958) 'remit' to supply Alexandra Dock engine shed with shunting locomotives, if and when required, Springhead had a handful of the 0-6-0Ts ready and waiting. On 4th August 1956 J72 No.69003 was one such engine allocated to 53C for the purposes of spending time at Alex Dock, if and when required! When BR came into being Springhead could muster twenty-odd 0-6-0 tank engines, the majority being J72 but five J77 and three J73 were also allocated. Note the stationery boiler with a chimney extension simply bolted to the existing chimney; the dome – minus cover – has a pipe connected for steam collection and the tank locomotive seconded to the duty appears to have its motion still in situ. Although there is no record of what locomotive was used at this time, it looks like an A7 Pacific tank which would not surprise this compiler because Springhead shed ended up with fifteen of that class – 75% – ending their days at 53C, only Nos.69770, 69773, 69775, 69777 and 69779 were withdrawn from another shed – Dairycoates! C.J.B.Sanderson (ARPT).

Well it wasn't this one was it? A7 No.69772 on the shed yard at Springhead on 4th August 1956. Note the painted-on 53C on the right centre of the smokebox door. The 4-6-2T had only been resident at Springhead since its transfer from Dairycoates on 27th November 1955. With the evidence already presented to us methinks a shortage of 53C shed plates was a fact. No.69772 was not condemned until 16th December 1957 so the shed plate saga must have been sorted before then! The target board reads S9. *C.J.B.Sanderson (ARPT).*

It would be rude to visit Springhead shed and not feature a Hull & Barnsley locomotive; luckily in the early 1950s there were still some survivors around such as N13 No.69119 seen at the eastern end of Springhead shed circa summer 1952. In November 1952 the 0-6-2T went to the works at Gateshead for a General overhaul, its last; a transfer to Neville Hill in September 1953 saw it join the remaining four members of the class in Leeds. When the last of the N13s – 69114 – was condemned on Monday 22nd October 1956, its passing also marked the end of the H&B locomotive contribution to Britain's railways. The corrugated iron clad building on the right was the hot water boiler washing plant, an LNER contribution to the more efficient workings of the depot. *K.H.Cockerill (ARPT)*.

J77 No.68402, another of the Alexandra Dock regulars which has come home for some R&R. These sturdy 0-6-0Ts were very powerful and ideal for pushing loaded coal wagons into the elevated staiths. Alexandra Dock had some from the 1930s when Hull was still exporting coal to continental Europe. Of course when wartime came all the coal exports ceased as did any coastal shipping down to the Thames. However, the J77 remained in Hull and were variously used by Alex Dock, Dairycoates, and Springhead. This undated image reveals that the six-coupled tank was wearing a 53C shed plate and it was allocated there from 8th September 1946 to 8th March 1953 when it transferred to Dairycoates. Therefore, the date was most probably at some time in 1952 when the J77 was between major overhauls and was not looking its best. Its move to 53A was not its last and in May 1954 it was sent to Tweedmouth. However, on 1st July 1956 it was called to North Blyth where for the next two years it barked its head off doing what it was designed for – pushing loaded mineral wagons onto the staiths. Now then, about the ventilation! *K.H.Cockerill (ARPT).*

Okay, let's spoil those H&B fans with another N13. This is No.69113 at the western end of Springhead shed yard on 18th October 1952; some three days after the following Christmas the 0-6-2T transferred to Neville Hill to join other class members which had been sent away to Leeds when Germany bombed Hull during World War Two. No.69113's sojourn at 55H was short and a trip to the works at Gateshead on 13th April 1953 saw it put to one side and three weeks later condemned. It was sent to Darlington for cutting up. What of other ex-H&B classes which survived the LNER? Class N12 nearly made it but the withdrawal of No.9089 on 30th August 1948 during a visit to Darlington saw that lot become history although it was only No.9089 which had survived the purges of the 1930s when the other eight of the nine N12 were condemned. Why that singleton survived into BR days isn't quite straightforward but it shunted the wagon works at Tuxford from November 1938 until January 1942 when it was called back to Springhead to do the same job at the C&W works. Class N11 was another small class of just five locomotives acquired by the H&B in unusual circumstances in February 1901 when Kitson & Co. had five new locomotives on their hands after the Lancashire, Derbyshire & East Coast Railway, who had ordered the engines, could not afford to pay for them. Step in the locomotive hungry H&B and everyone was happy! The two-storey brick building on the right was the Oil store! Behind the N13 is the overhead water storage for the water softener located beneath it; there was another water storage tank behind that. A visit to the site of Springhead engine shed today would be somewhat difficult to digest as it is virtually impossible to define where anything was, shed or works! *C.J.B.Sanderson (ARPT)*.

53C SUB - ALEXANDRA DOCK

A nostalgic view of the shed-cum-stabling point at Alexandra Dock on 4th April 1954 with thirteen 0-6-0T shunters from varying classes stabled for the Sunday break. The location of the depot at the eastern end of the north side quay of Alexandra Dock was visible from Hedon Road but this image was captured from the ramp carrying the track up to the coal hoist or tippler – from the days when Hull was one of the largest coal exporting ports in the country. The time, according to the shadows, is circa midday and so it will be a few hours yet before the firelighter starts his rounds of the tank engines to get them ready for Monday morning and another week of shunting these docks. Only two of the engines are carrying targets, No.54 on the 0-6-0T alongside the coaling stage and No.53 on the rear of the engine by the embankment. Just two locomotive numbers are visible, both J72s: Nos.68753 and 68747. The J72 represented the largest class at Alexandra Dock with more than dozen examples allocated. These were in addition to a handful of J73, five or so J77, and a single N13; the latter used mainly for tripping to the railway yards. From May 1937 J72 No.68747 had completed five different periods of allocation to Alex Dock shed, this most recent one starting on 24th January 1954 and ending on 22nd August 1954 when the 0-6-0T transferred to Heaton; it never returned to Hull and ended its days at Tyne Dock shed on 23rd October 1961, an old sea dog to the end! Sister No.68753 spent virtually the whole of its life working from Alexandra Dock shed starting on Christmas Eve 1925 (a two-month stint at Selby in summer 1940 can be overlooked!) until transferred away to Dairycoates in May 1954. Nos.1 and 2 graving docks both have customers on the stocks but alas we have no record of the names of the freighters. *F.W.Hampson (ARPT).*

From virtually the same camera position photographer Gordon Turner captured this view of the Alexandra Dock depot in the 1960s. Steam has long gone, the coaling stage is bereft of coal and diesel shunters now rule the docks. We have twelve locomotives on view and they are made up of what was to become TOPS Classes 03, 08, and 11. Identifiable are Nos.12119, D2169, and D2157. Although the 'shed' here was a sub to Springhead, following on from Hull & Barnsley Railway days, the shunting locomotives were all supplied by Dairycoates and their 'pool' of shunting diesels consisted the following during the period when this image was likely captured on film in the early 1960s: 204 h.p. 0-6-0DM – D2051 to D2054, D2064, D2065, D2081, D2098, D2100 to D2102, D2151, D2155 to D2157, D2168 to D2174, D2268; 350 h.p. 0-6-0DE – D3070 to D3081, D3139 to D3143, D3230 to D3236, D3313, D3318, D3323, D3675, D3676, D3944, D3945, and 12113 to 12122. Throughout the LNER and BR periods the shunting locomotives were actually listed as allocated to Alexandra Dock engine shed but on 27th October 1963 they were all re-allocated to Dairycoates (did someone realised there hadn't been a shed building there for the past thirty-odd years?) although they remained stabled on this site for a few more years. Note the 50B shed plates attached to the centre of the cab lower rear panel on each diesel. Neither plate is central to the 'wasp stripes' with one to the left and the other to the right – modellers beware! It is interesting to note that the majority of the shunters are facing east, only two of them 'bucking the trend.' Targets are now Nos.94 and 96, the numbers used by engines working King George Dock next door; no doubt some of the hidden targets would be in the 50-59 number group. Note the lack of shipping using the graving docks. *Gordon Turner (ARPT).*

Another aspect of the Alex Dock depot: The date is 18th May 1952 – a Sunday – and as usual the sun is shining on Hull. From the vantage point of the coal hoist incline our photographer has recorded the quiet side of the site with the depot's two breakdown and accident vans on show. This compiler is not too sure of the origin of either van but the notes say that the nearest vehicle is ex-HB&WRJR – Hull Barnsley & West Riding Junction Railway. The legend on its lower side states – LOCO DEPT ALEXANDRA DOCK HULL. The faded fleet number is DE90167 whilst the plate on the solebar bears No.901622. It looks like a riding and stores van but I'm open to suggestions! The second van has the same location data but its fleet number is DE90553; the solebar plate is indiscernible. Standing alone on the stage road is one of the Consolidated fleet coal wagons which carries the number 725; its coal load appears to a reasonable batch considering the period when the NCB was having difficulty extracting decent coal from most of its collieries. The graving docks are back in business but note we have gone back in time! *C.J.B.Sanderson (ARPT).*

This undated but obviously early BR view is included to show the exact location of the wooden, two-road shed which was removed in 1927 after years of dereliction had taken its toll. The wagon on the extreme left, attached to a hand crane, stands on one of the two roads which – as can just be made out – were equipped with inspection pits. During Hull & Barnsley days the area now covered by the tracks used for locomotive stabling and also for the coaling stage, used to be a timber yard. The former shed site was taken over by the CME and the wood yard became the new locomotive depot site. A 130ft long inspection pit was provided along with a 60ft ash pit next to the coal stage; the capacity of the latter for storage purposes was some 50-tons! Other facilities included a small fitting shop with oil store, mess room, time and foreman's office, and a sand furnace. Quite self-contained! Locomotives on show include J72 No.69001 (resident 31st October 1949 to 26th June 1955), J77 No.68429 (resident 27th September 1937 to 24th January 1954). Although only half a dozen engines are stabled, they are all facing east. *D.R.Dunn collection (ARPT).*

Animation at Alexandra Dock with J72 Nos.69010 and 69009 preparing to move the goods about the docks! Targets 54 and 55 were both listed as: Period required – 0600 Monday to 0600 Sunday, Shunting to be carried out as required. The image is undated but the J72s were both at Alexandra Dock shed until 13th November 1960 when they went to Dairycoates. Note that both engines carry the new BR crest on their tank sides and they each received such at General overhauls at Darlington as follows: 69009 – 19th November to 22nd December 1959; 69010 – 27th May to 22nd June 1959. Therefore, 1960 would be a fairly accurate assumption for a year; now as for a month and day?? *D.R.Dunn collection (ARPT).*

This undated image shows two of the J77s allocated to Alexandra Dock depot, Nos.68401 and E8402, taking a break between duties. No.68401 was resident at the sub-shed from 17th October 1948 (ex-York) until 11th September 1949 when it transferred to Dairycoates. No.E8402 had been resident from 8th September 1946 (also ex-York) until 8th March 1953 when Dairycoates became the recipient. To pin down the date of the image further, the E prefix was added to the number during a 'General' on 20th February 1948; it disappeared in December 1950 when 60000 was added to the number. Note that a front number plate was also waiting to be added not to mention BR emblems, etc., the latter was relevant to 68401 also. So, we have a date at some time in 1949. Target No.98 was a King George Dock shunt which had been abolished by 1951. The building forming the background is the hydraulic engine house. *D.R.Dunn collection.*

Does anyone know where the shed is?! A party of thirty-odd enthusiasts have slipped off their road transport and have entered the precincts of Alexandra Dock looking for the non-existent shed with its elusive little shunting engines. If you were from anywhere other than Hull, the dozen or so engines hiding in here became something of a treasure hunt to find. It is nice to see the ease with which these non-railway beings walked around the premises without hard-hats, conspicu'ity coats, special glasses, but perhaps more importantly without injury! Right, you've got fifteen minutes before the coach goes! Fifteen! It's down there, about a mile away! What!! Alexandra Dock signal box dated from the 1920s and was designated as an HB1 type; with 97 levers, the box was replaced in 1958 by a new box having 91 levers. The replacement only lasted until the end of May 1974. *J.W.Armstrong (ARPT).*

Every picture tells a story: Bridlington engine shed Sunday 12th July 1959. It appears as though there is room to spare as Dairycoates K3 No.61932 shunts some stock on the left. There was a surprising variety of visitors on this day with Woodford Halse K3 No.61841 probably taking the accolade for most distant shed (but not the cleaning prize); just to its left Stanier Cl.5 No.44932 from Agecroft had brought an excursion – 957 – from Manchester (Victoria), it too was not exactly pristine externally. Next one identifiable was Thompson B1 No.61111 which had brought an excursion (337) from Sheffield. Then it was sister No.61036 RALPH ASSHETON, one of Doncaster's longest serving but not cleanest B1s which worked in on No.351. Finally in the identified lot comes No.60855 which was taking water; this York based V2 had completed a General overhaul in late January 1959 when separate cylinders and ATC were fitted. The 2-6-2 had also had a complete repaint but that fact is lost beneath the grime. B16s and other B1s were stabled but their numbers are lost in time. Such were the summer weekends at Bridlington 1959-65, an engine shed which, on paper, did not exist! *N.W.Skinner (ARPT).*

The shape of things to come! Bridlington 4th April 1954. Not an engine in sight on this Sunday morning but this image helps us track down the probable date when the 55ft turntable was installed. The two four-wheel coaches are interesting and may well have constituted a breakdown train of sorts. Note the tiny coaling platform located at the corner of the shed. The stage doesn't look as though it could hold much more than a ton of coal; perhaps it was there simply to serve the two Sentinel shunters which once graced the shed intermittently. For anybody modelling this place it is worth noting the lighting conductor which is quite prominent on that front gable. Now does anyone know why those four bollards stand near the end columns of the shed? Answers please, to the usual address! *F.W.Hampson (ARPT).*

Direct trains ran to Bridlington from the industrial heartlands via Selby and Market Weighton in the summer, mainly at weekends but some mid-week traffic existed albeit small in comparison. As the resort expanded the station also grew and in 1912 a wide concourse was built and longer, albeit curved, platforms were provided. After World War One excursion platforms (Nos.7&8) were added to the original six platforms (now only platforms 4, 5, and 6 remain – 4 & 5 serving the through lines with No.6 as a terminal bay, the rest having been demolished). Like a lot of stations nowadays, Bridlington is manned part-time, a radical change from the heyday of pre-war and post-war summers. This is the engine shed circa 1956 shortly after the 'new' turntable was installed. Ex-LNER types dominate but at least three former-LMS engines accounted for some of the smoke polluting the seaside air. Only Stanier Cl.5 No.44839 is identified, it's reporting number M893 posted on the tender temporarily. Assuming this is 1956, the Class 5 was allocated to Derby. Part of the small coaling platform mentioned opposite can the seen on the right. *K.H.Cockerill (ARPT)*.

Late afternoon on Sunday 6th August 1961 with a mainly ex-LNER locomotive stud stabled awaiting return excursions. We can see three Thompson B1s, a Gresley K3, a Stanier Cl.5 and a BR Standard Cl.5. However, we only have the following identified: Nos.61327 (Darnall on 1F94), 61139 (Darnall on 1F98), 61857 (Dairycoates – this K3 had spent its whole life working in Scotland until February 1957 when it transferred to Hull), and 73166 (Huddersfield). The shed had been closed for nearly three years and it was as busy as ever; note how neat and tidy the place appeared! *N.W.Skinner (ARPT)*.

The date is 19th June 1960 a Sunday of course and the early afternoon sun highlights the dirt ridden hulk of Patricroft based BR Standard Caprotti Class 5 No.73130. The 4-6-0 has brought an excursion from Manchester (Exchange) [216] and is turned and serviced ready for the evening return. The tender carried seven tons of coal, enough (just) for the journey back over the Pennines via the Standedge route. Alongside is B1 No.61021 REITBOK which had come from the Wakefield area. *N.W.Skinner (ARPT)*.

One of the problems of the summer Sunday throng was the smoke especially when the locomotives were being prepared for their departures in the evening. This undated but circa 1956 view from Bessingby Road bridge shows a full house being got ready whilst somebody is working out the sequence of departure not just from the shed but also from the carriage sidings and eventually the station. Most of the signal staff in Bridlington South signal box would have been on overtime but they were about to earn every penny. B1s, B16s, K3s, and a few ex-LMS types are amongst the twenty-nine engines in the image; more were inside the shed! We mustn't forget the resident locomotives which comprised nine locomotives in circa 1951 thus: D20 – 62353, 62355, 62375; D49 – 62703, 62707, 62750, 62766; Y1 – 68148; Y3 – 68155 (the year before some ten locomotives were allocated). Others came later, A5s, G5s, L1s, N8s, LMS Cl.3 2-6-2T, BR Standard Cl.3 2-6-0; some on loan from Hull Botanic Gardens where their presence was not required during the shed rebuilding there. It was one of the BR Standards – No.77010 – which was the last steam locomotive to be allocated (albeit on loan), vacating the premises in September 1958. *K.H.Cockerill (ARPT).*

(*above*) A rather dated photograph from a sunny summer morning in the 1930s reveals a couple of interesting items of note. On the left is Sentinel railcar No.2245 which transferred into Bridlington from Botanic Gardens on 2nd February 1931. It was the only one of its kind to work here but moved away to Neville Hill in April 1941. We can see a tender engine inside the shed but have no idea what it might be. To the right is a ramp of which nothing is known but one possible use made of the structure was to run barrow loads of coal up to the Sentinels coal bunker. Any other suggestions or indeed actual knowledge of the origins of the ramp and its purpose would be gratefully accepted by the compiler via the usual channels please. *J.W.Armstrong miscellany (ARPT)*. (right) The miniature signal protecting the shed exit at Bridlington; 6th August 1961. It would have been nice to have something to compare alongside. *N.W.Skinner (ARPT)*.

(*right*) **Miniature Signal shed exit**

This view of the depot on 16th June 1963 shows the normal disposition of Bridlington throughout the year excepting the weekends during the summer months of July, August and early September. Once the last of the visitors has gone home, the water column was turned off and allowed to drain so there was no requirement for a 'fire-devil' during those months when temperatures hovered or dipped below 32 degrees Fahrenheit. The turntable is not the original 50ft unit which was located virtually against the retaining wall of Station Road beyond the elevated water tank and dated from 1892. The new unit is one of the 55ft appliances provided by British Railways circa 1955/6 – the turntable was actually second-hand and salvaged from somewhere on the system whereas the pit was at least new! Not much happened at Bridlington but when it did it could be quite spectacular as was the case on Tuesday 27th May 1958 when Botanic Gardens based D49 No.62703 HERTFORDSHIRE fell into the turntable pit. Recovery was eventually attained but the 4-4-0 was badly damaged and was taken off to Darlington where it was scrapped. The D49 was no stranger to the shed yard as it was allocated to 53D from November 1950 until September 1957 when it transferred to Hull. Note that the shed building is in remarkable condition considering it was some 70-years old at this date but the place had hardly been used throughout its normal life and only during those summer weekends was it anything like full to capacity. Its allocation when the LNER came into being was just seven locomotives, all D22 class 4-4-0 tender engines. When BR took over twenty-five years later only five locomotives were allocated and two of those were little Sentinel 0-4-0s, the others were three D20s! There never was any coaling facility here other than open wagons, brawn and shovels. So, the 'foreign' crews in-the-know topped up their charges before leaving home. It might have been noted by some of you that the only apparent illumination in this part of the shed yard was the single gas lamp by the water column; two others were located on the corner of the shed and one on a standard overlooking the turntable pit. *N.W.Skinner (ARPT).*

Not having an image of the actual incident from that Tuesday in May 1958, we present this illustration of the bruised and doomed D49 at Darlington Works Crossing on 6th July 1958. *C.W.Allen (ARPT)*.

The inevitable occurred in May 1966 when BR started to dismantle the infrastructure of the shed yard. Starting inside the shed, the rails were lifted and then the outside rails on the 30ft pits; white painted warning slabs have been laid on Nos.2 and 3 roads, and red flags placed on metal spikes. The lifting on No.1 road is more advanced but note concrete sleepers on all three shed road – now when did they go in? The eagle-eyed will have spotted the clock on the rear wall inside the shed, the time is showing 4-10 p.m. (1610) which coincides somewhat with the position of the sun on this the 28th day of May. On the right the water tower stands taller than originally planned courtesy of an extension placed atop the cast tank of circa 1892. To finish off this piece on Bridlington, and indeed the album on the Hull district engine sheds, we note on the left, leaving the station, a diesel hauled passenger train with one of the BR Sulzer Type 2 Bo-Bo diesel-electric locomotives *N.W.Skinner (ARPT)*.